SPIRIT

A book of happiness for horse lovers

EXISLE
PUBLISHING

Introduction

Horses. From the smallest pony to the largest draft horse, our equine friends possess a nobility of spirit and a timeless wisdom that horse lovers everywhere instinctively recognize.

There are few places where we can feel more alive than when admiring the view from a horse's back. There are few places we can feel more understood than when breathing in their warm scent as we brush their coat until it shines.

Horses teach us responsibility, consistency and patience. Our relationships with them are built on trust over time. They live in the moment, always fully present. They take us as they find us on any given day. All they ask is that we do the same.

Whether in the showjumping arena, out on a trail ride, mustering cattle, or simply galloping wild, horses are the epitome of grace and power. From a little girl's first pony to a gnarled cowboy's

last quarter horse, they have an ability to touch our souls and connect with our hearts in a way that few other animals can. They offer us some of our deepest friendships and inspire us to be the best version of ourselves.

It's not surprising, therefore, that horses have inspired memorable quotes across the centuries. Saint Augustine, Winston Churchill, Nathaniel Hawthorne, William Faulkner, Dale Carnegie and Ralph Waldo Emerson are just a few of the famous names who've been inspired to comment on our equine companions.

The quotes collected here are not all by famous people, however; nor are they all deep and meaningful. After all, as anyone who's been nudged by a playful pony knows, horses aren't just about grace and power — there's plenty of mischief there too!

The essential joy of being with horses is that it brings us in contact with the rare elements of grace, beauty, spirit and fire.

SHARON RALLS LEMON

Horses and children, I often think, have a lot of the good sense there is in the world.

JOSEPHINE DEMOTT ROBINSON

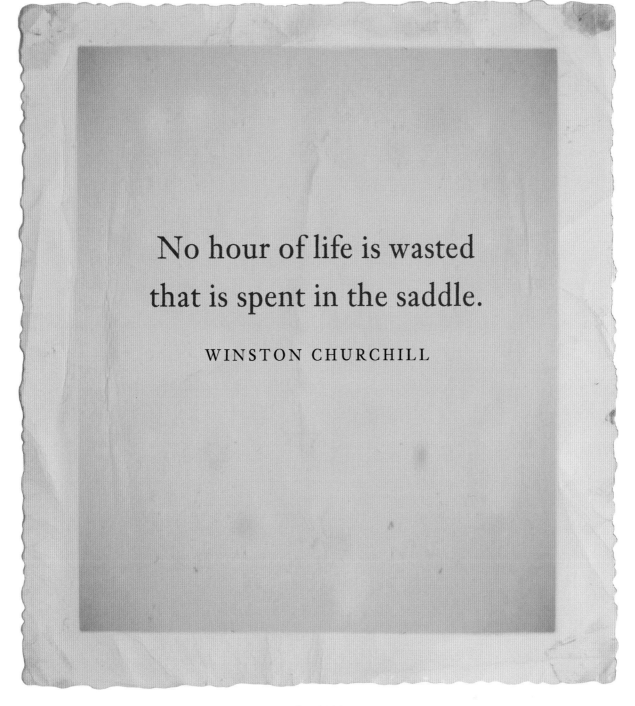

No hour of life is wasted
that is spent in the saddle.

WINSTON CHURCHILL

There is no secret so close
as that between a rider
and his horse.

ROBERT SMITH SURTEES

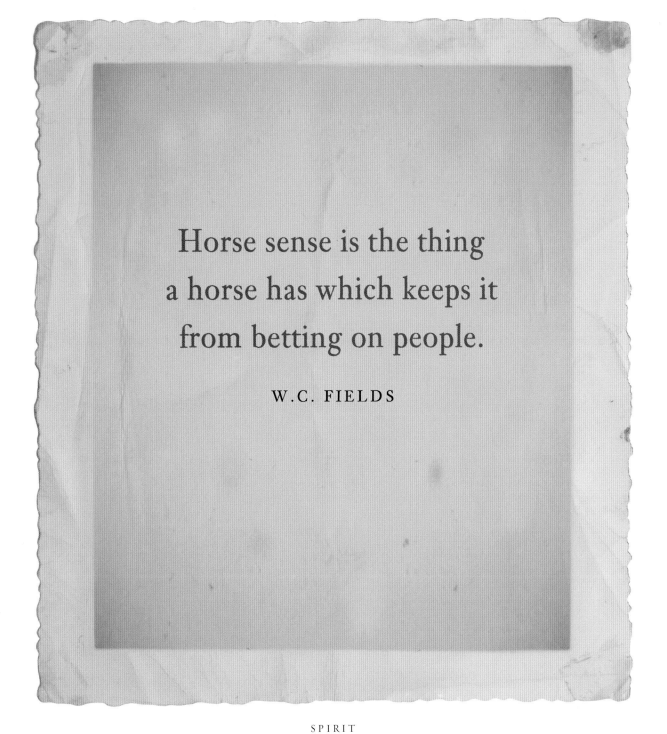

Horse sense is the thing
a horse has which keeps it
from betting on people.

W.C. FIELDS

The wagon rests in winter, the sleigh in summer, the horse never.

YIDDISH PROVERB

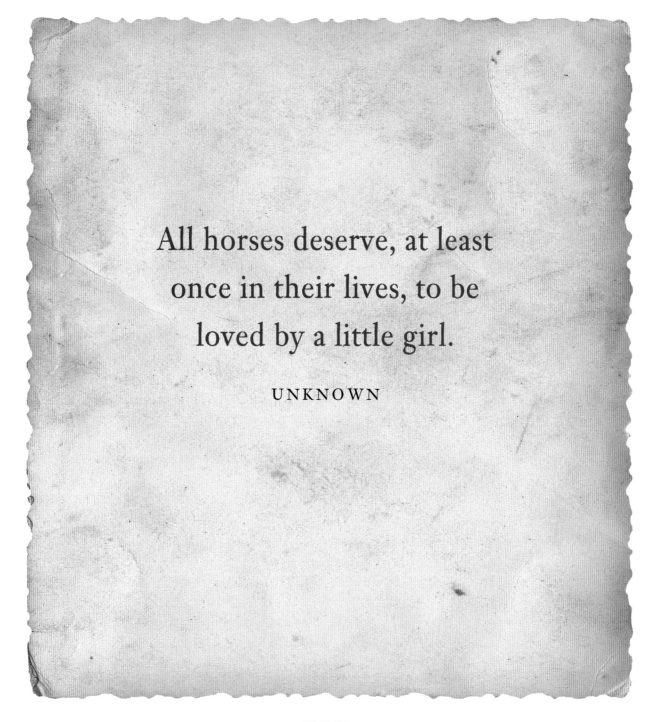

All horses deserve, at least
once in their lives, to be
loved by a little girl.

UNKNOWN

He knows when you're happy.

He knows when you're comfortable.

He knows when you're confident.

And he *always* knows when you have carrots.

UNKNOWN

The wind of heaven is that which blows between a horse's ears.

ARABIAN PROVERB

To ride a horse is to ride the sky.

UNKNOWN

The horse. Here is nobility without conceit, friendship without envy, beauty without vanity. A willing servant, yet never a slave.

RONALD DUNCAN

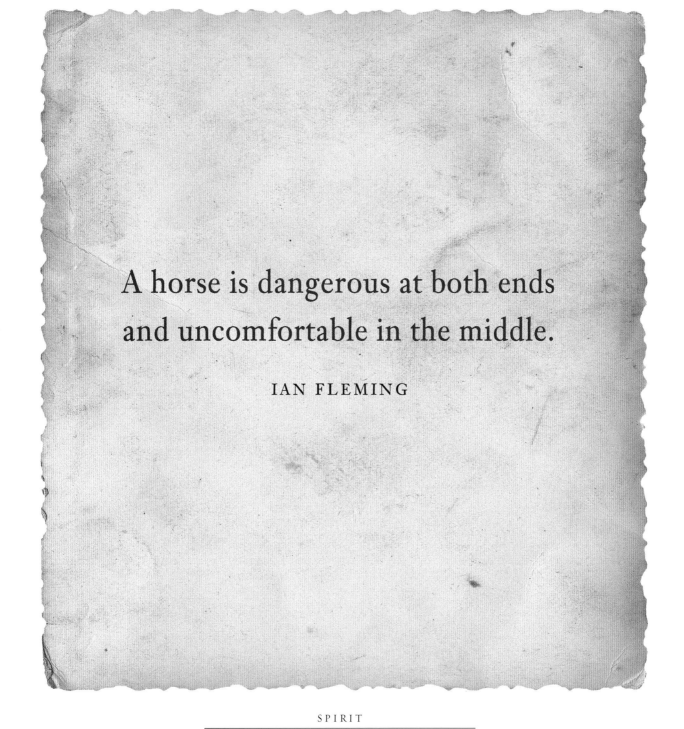

A horse is dangerous at both ends
and uncomfortable in the middle.

IAN FLEMING

There is nothing so good for the inside of a man as the outside of a horse.

JOHN LUBBOCK

A horse is the projection of peoples' dreams about themselves — strong, powerful, beautiful — and it has the capability of giving us escape from our mundane existence.

PAM BROWN

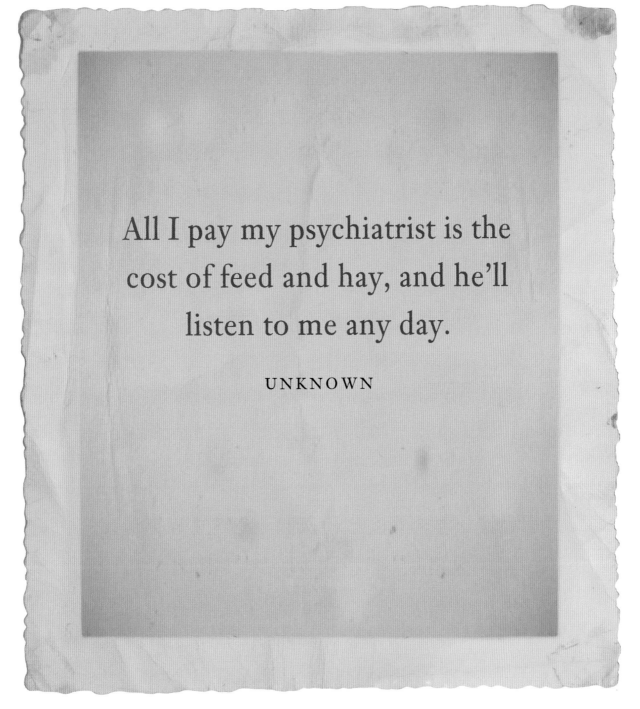

All I pay my psychiatrist is the cost of feed and hay, and he'll listen to me any day.

UNKNOWN

Silence takes on a new
quality when the only
sound is that of regular
and smooth hoof beats.

BERTRAND LECLAIR

A Hibernian sage once wrote
that there are three things a
man never forgets: the girl
of his early youth, a devoted
teacher, and a great horse.

C.J.J. MULLEN

A canter is a cure for every evil.

BENJAMIN DISRAELI

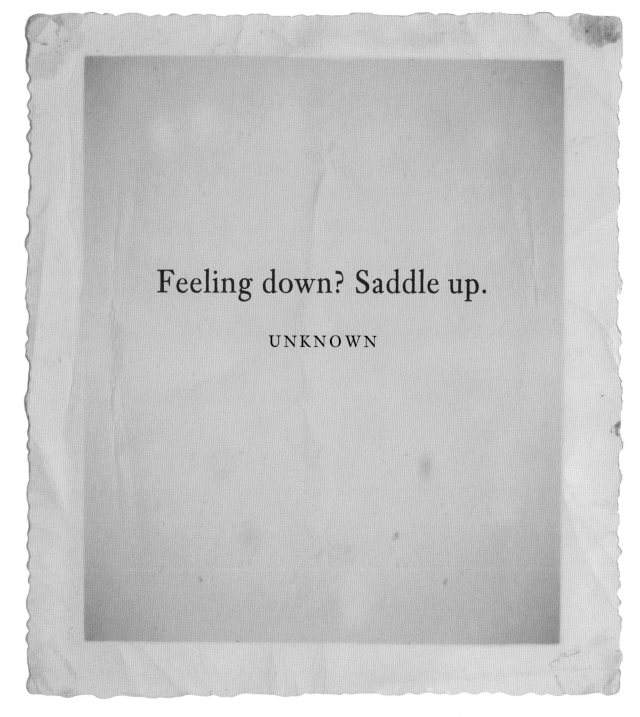

Feeling down? Saddle up.

UNKNOWN

A horse is worth more
than riches.

SPANISH PROVERB

Wherever man has left his
footprint in the long ascent
from barbarism to civilization
we will find the hoofprint of
the horse beside it.

JOHN MOORE

Small children are
convinced that ponies
deserve to see the inside
of the house.

MAYA PATEL

A horse can lend its rider
the speed and strength he
or she lacks, but the rider
who is wise remembers it
is no more than a loan.

PAM BROWN

One reason why birds and horses are not unhappy is because they are not trying to impress other birds and horses.

DALE CARNEGIE

Spending that many hours in the saddle gave a man plenty of time to think. That's why so many cowboys fancied themselves Philosophers.

CHARLES M. RUSSELL

If your horse says no, you either
asked the wrong question, or
asked the question wrong.

PAT PARELLI

Gypsy gold does not chink and glitter. It gleams in the sun and neighs in the dark.

CLADDAGH GYPSIES OF GALWAY

Horses — if God made anything more beautiful, he kept it for himself.

UNKNOWN

If you want a stable friendship,
get a horse.

UNKNOWN

And Allah took a handful
of southerly wind, blew
his breath over it, and
created the horse ... Thou
shall fly without wings,
and conquer without any
sword, oh horse.

BEDOUIN LEGEND

Men are generally more careful of the breed of their horses and dogs than of their children.

WILLIAM PENN

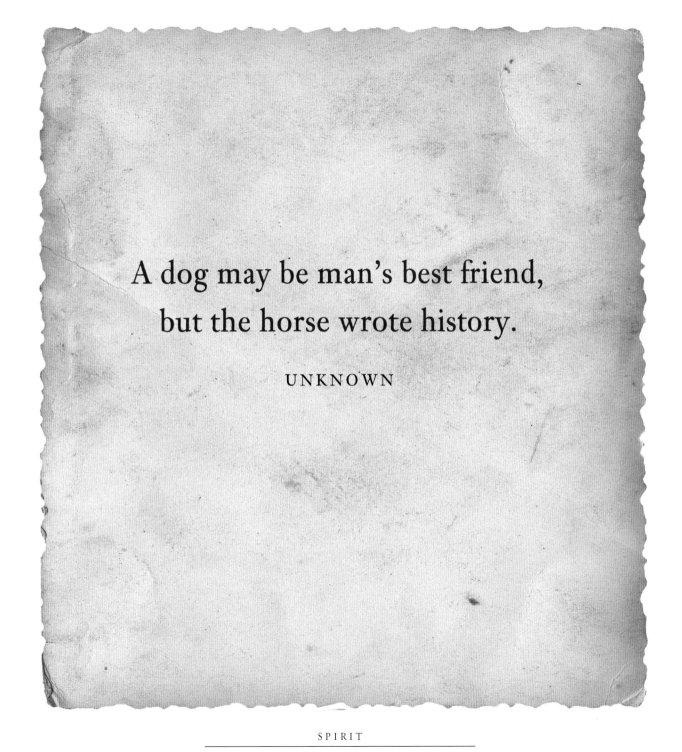

A dog may be man's best friend,
but the horse wrote history.

UNKNOWN

A man on a horse is spiritually
as well as physically bigger
than a man on foot.

JOHN STEINBECK

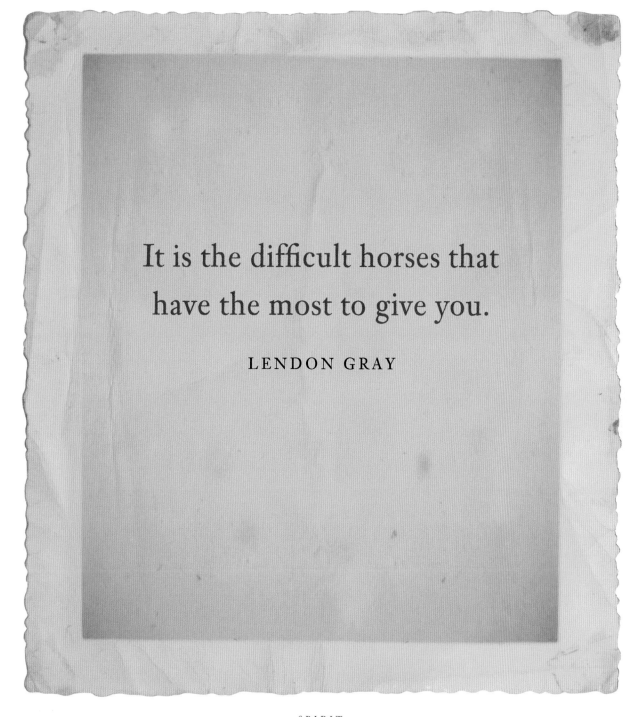

It is the difficult horses that
have the most to give you.

LENDON GRAY

What the colt learns
in youth, he continues
in old age.

FRENCH PROVERB

A horseman should know
neither fear nor anger.

JAMES RAREY

Words are as beautiful as
wild horses, and sometimes as
difficult to corral.

TED BERKMAN

Horses are the dolphins of the plains, the spirits of the wind; yet we sit astride them for the sake of being well-groomed, whereas they could have all the desire in the world to bolt, but instead, they adjust their speed and grace only to please us, never to displease.

LAUREN SALERNO

A stubborn horse walks behind you, an impatient horse walks in front of you, but a noble companion walks beside you.

UNKNOWN

Bread may feed my body,
but my horse feeds my soul.

ARABIAN PROVERB

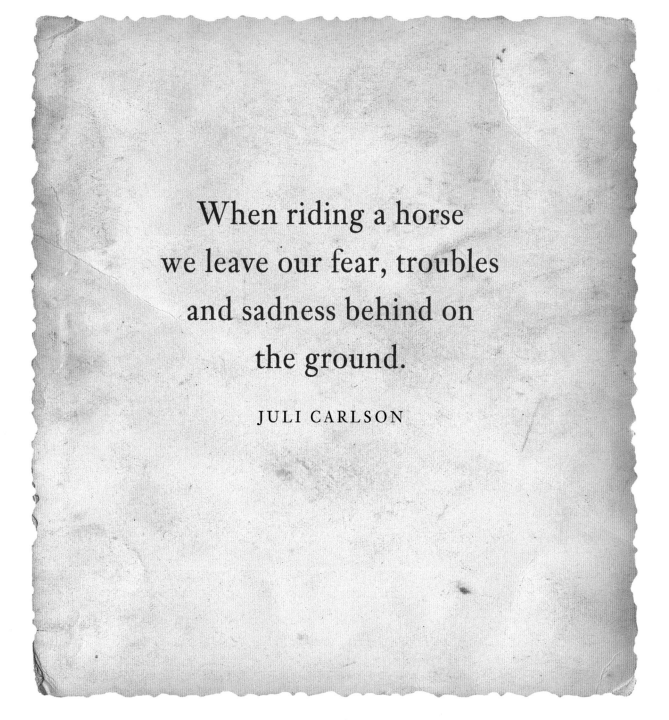

When riding a horse
we leave our fear, troubles
and sadness behind on
the ground.

JULI CARLSON

A horse never runs so fast as
when he has other horses to
catch up and outpace.

OVID

An equestrian is never alone,
is always sensing the other
being, the mysterious but
also understandable living
being that is the horse.

JANE SMILEY

I call horses 'divine mirrors'
— they reflect back the
emotions you put in. If you
put in love and respect and
kindness and curiosity, the
horse will return that.

ALLAN HAMILTON

A horse is a thing of beauty ...
none will tire of looking at
him as long as he displays
himself in his splendour.

XENOPHON

The daughter who won't lift a finger in the house is the same child who cycles madly off in the pouring rain to spend all morning mucking out a stable.

SAMANTHA ARMSTRONG

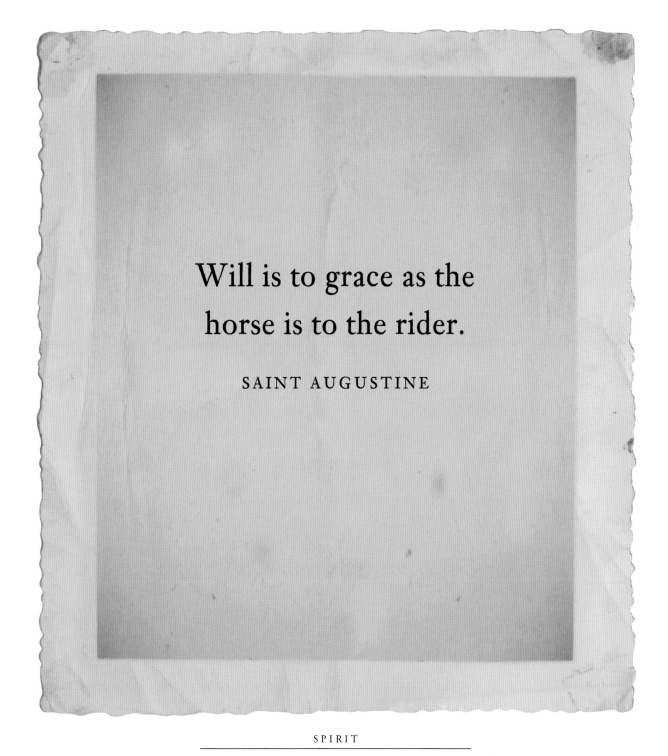

Will is to grace as the
horse is to the rider.

SAINT AUGUSTINE

There is something about jumping
a horse over a fence, something
that makes you feel good. Perhaps
it's the risk, the gamble. In any
event, it's a thing I need.

WILLIAM FAULKNER

In riding a horse, we borrow freedom.

HELEN THOMPSON

Never approach a bull from the
front, a horse from the rear, or
a fool from any direction.

COWBOY SAYING

God forbid that I should go to any heaven in which there are no horses.

R.B. CUNNINGHAME-GRAHAM

A pony is a childhood dream,
a horse is an adulthood treasure.

REBECCA CARROLL

Honour lies in the mane
of a horse.

HERMAN MELVILLE

Sell the cow, buy the sheep,
but never be without the horse.

IRISH PROVERB

As a horse runs, think of it as
a game of tag with the wind.

TRE TUBERVILLE

Whether you regard the
horse with awe or love,
it is impossible to escape the
sheer power of his presence.

MARY WANLESS

Closeness, friendship, affection:
keeping your own horse means
all these things.

BERTRAND LECLAIR

I've spent most of my life riding horses. The rest I've just wasted.

UNKNOWN

I heard a neigh. Oh, such a brisk and melodious neigh as that was! My very heart leaped with delight at the sound.

NATHANIEL HAWTHORNE

I am still under the impression
that there is nothing alive quite
so beautiful as a thoroughbred horse.

JOHN GALSWORTHY

Riding a horse is not a
gentle hobby, to be picked
up and laid down like a
game of Solitaire.
It is a grand passion.

RALPH WALDO EMERSON

A horse doesn't care how
much you know until he
knows how much you care.

PAT PARELLI

A horse will cross any bridge
you build as long as the first
one is from him to you.

UNKNOWN

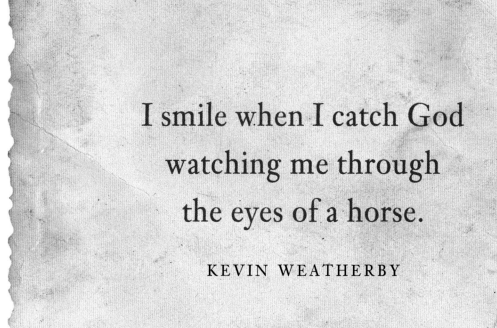

I smile when I catch God
watching me through
the eyes of a horse.

KEVIN WEATHERBY

Ask me to show you poetry
in motion, and I will show
you a horse.

UNKNOWN

The horseman allows the horse to keep his dignity and the horse still likes the horseman in the end.

JESSE WESTFALL

The best horse doesn't
always win the race.

IRISH PROVERB

To know him as he really is, we must watch him under the open sky, in the meadow, among his own kind, for there we can see how different each horse is from his companions, how the ancient law of the herd lives on, and how the hierarchy is created with barely an encounter.

HANS-HEINRICH ISENBART

Show me your horse and
I will tell you what you are.

ENGLISH PROVERB

The wildest colts make
the best horses.

PLUTARCH

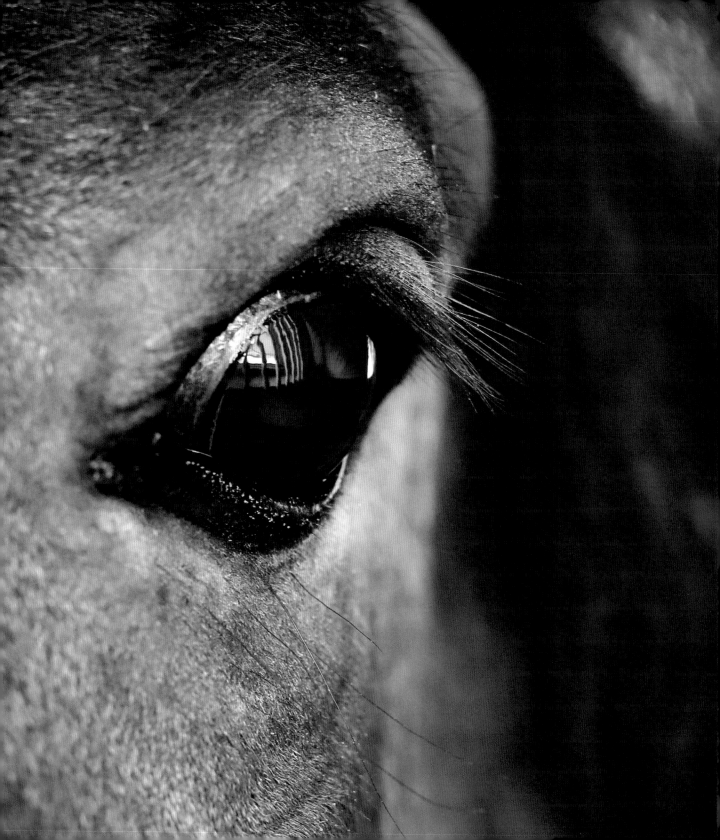

A dog looks up to a man.
A cat looks down on a man.
But a patient horse looks
a man in the eye and sees
him as an equal.

UNKNOWN

Horses know how to be loyal
but still keep their distance.

SADIE JONES

A horse which stops dead just before a jump and thus propels its rider into a graceful arc provides a splendid excuse for general merriment.

PRINCE PHILIP, DUKE OF EDINBURGH

A lovely horse is always
an experience … It is an
emotional experience of the
kind that is spoiled by words.

BERYL MARKHAM

There are friends and faces
that may be forgotten, but there
are horses that never will be.

ANDY ADAMS

The sight of him did something to me I've never quite been able to explain. He was more than tremendous speed and beauty of motion. He set me dreaming.

WALT MOREY

I have seen things so beautiful they have brought tears to my eyes. Yet none of them can match the gracefulness and beauty of a horse running free.

UNKNOWN

Also by Exisle Publishing …

MEOW

A book of happiness for cat lovers

ANOUSKA JONES

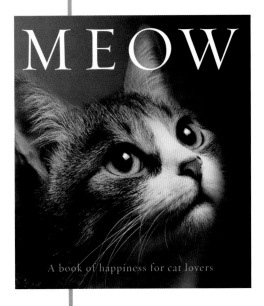

Cats have a way of walking into our lives and making themselves right at home. No cat lover can imagine life without a feline presence — even if it is only as fleeting as the occasional conversation with a neighbourhood stray.

Meow: A book of happiness for cat lovers is a compendium of delightful quotes that capture the essence of this fascination. Some are by famous people (Mark Twain, Jean Cocteau, Ernest Hemingway), others not; some are philosophical, others light-hearted — all are memorable.

Beautifully designed and featuring high-quality photography, this companion volume to *Woof* is a collection of quotes to treasure.

ISBN 978 1 925335 08 8

WOOF

A book of happiness for dog lovers

ANOUSKA JONES

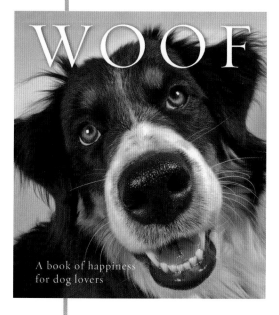

Dogs make our lives feel complete. They're there for us through good times and bad, with their wholehearted engagement in life a lesson to us all on 'living in the moment'.

This companion volume to *Meow* is the perfect gift for any dog lover, with its selection of quotes ranging from the serious to the light-hearted, accompanied by beautiful photography.

ISBN 978 1 925335 57 6

First published 2017

Exisle Publishing Pty Ltd
PO Box 864, Chatswood, NSW 2057, Australia
226 High Street, Dunedin, 9016, New Zealand
www.exislepublishing.com

A CiP record for this book is available from the National Library of Australia.

ISBN 978 1 925335 51 4

Designed by Big Cat Design
Typeset in Archetype 24 on 36pt
Photographs courtesy of Shutterstock
Printed in China

This book uses paper sourced under ISO 14001 guidelines from well-managed forests and other controlled sources.

4 6 8 10 9 7 5 3